Garabed Nergarian

A Brief History of the Beginning of the Mission Work in

Nicomedia by the American Board of Foreign Missions

Garabed Nergarian

A Brief History of the Beginning of the Mission Work in Nicomedia by the American Board of Foreign Missions

ISBN/EAN: 9783744781138

Printed in Europe, USA, Canada, Australia, Japan

Cover: Foto ©ninafisch / pixelio.de

More available books at **www.hansebooks.com**

A

BRIEF HISTORY

OF THE

BEGINNING

OF THE

MISSION WORK

IN

NICOMEDIA

BY THE

AMERICAN BOARD OF FOREIGN MISSIONS.

—   —

By REV. GARABED NERGARARIAN.

WAYNESBORO, PA.:
GAZETTE STEAM PRINTING HOUSE.
1885.

PREFACE.

Under the Missionaries sent out by the American Board of Foreign Missions, the parents of the Author of this brief sketch were among the first converts, hence he himself grew up with the work, as it were, and, in his early life, became identified with it.   He taught school in his native city, Nicomedia, for several years, after which time he entered a Seminary in Asia Minor, where he graduated.   He was then sent out as a native Missionary by the American Board.   He was greatly blessed in his labors and succeeded in establishing a church in which he was ordained by the missionaries as a minister.   In this capacity he labored for eight years.

Having a great desire for self-improvement, in order that he might better serve his people, he was induced to come to America for further study and the acquiring of a knowledge of English, since this opens up an avenue to so many commentaries and books of Biblical reference.   Since his arrival in America he spent a little more than two years at Princeton Theological Seminary.   During the past year he has been in attendance at the Theological Seminary at Gettysburg.

This brief history of Missionary work has been written at the request of his many friends in America.   Much of the information herein contained was received from his parents, and many things have been written from his own personal knowledge.

As it is his purpose to return to his native home as soon as he can perfect his arrangements to that end, he wishes to leave this little book in America as a memento to his many kind friends.

WAYNESBORO, PA., September 1, 1885.

NICOMEDIA.

Nicomedia, historically, holds a prominent place in church history concerning the first period of the Christian Church. At present this city is generally known among the Turks by the name of Ismid.

With reference to the name Ismid there is a tradition current among the Turks which is as follows : Many years ago. when the Turks first became the conquerors of this country, one city after another was taken by them except Nicomedia which was very strongly fortified. By them the city was besieged for two years, yet it showed no signs of surrender. They then employed a stratagem to effect their purpose. Some sections of the country were then (as now) noted for their numerous flocks of goats, and the commander hit upon the happy thought of employing these to accomplish his purpose. Causing many thousands of them to be brought together upon a certain night he had candles tied to their horns and caused them to be driven from the Turkish camp, which was below the city, on the plains along the sea shore, towards the city. The defenders of the city seeing in the distance the great light made by these goats with their candles, and observing their rapid approach, became greatly alarmed, and all hastened forward to defend that part of the city where they expected the supposed attack, leaving the northern part almost entirely defenceless. The Turkish commander, in the mean time, took advantage of this carelessness on their part and entered the city before the people became aware of the deception. A most fearful and bloody struggle ensued, in which the Turks came off victorious. The Turkish commander, however, seeing that so many of his best soldiers were sacrificed in this terrible engagement, angrily cried out, "Ism e-it!" Hence the name, Ismid. *Ism-e* signifies *the name of*, and *it, dog*.

Just at the upper part of the city, at the place where the conquerors entered, is built a mosque in memory of Sultan Ochran who is supposed to be the victor of the city.

Back of the city, behind the hill, is a large Turkish cemetery, in which are buried those who are said to have fallen in this battle. It is for this reason called by them the "Cemetery of the Martyrs."

Nicomedia, the former capital of Bithynia, was one of the grandest and most flourishing cities of the old world. It is noted for its once having contained the Imperial residence of Constantine, Galerius, Julius,* and others. It receives its name from Nicomedes I. The city was seven times visited

---

*In the early days of the writer's father, there existed ruins of the palace of Julius (called Julius the wicked). Upon these ruins the boys of the neighborhood used to have their play grounds. Sultan Mahmoud II. built a beautiful palace (kiosk) upon the sight of these ruins. The materials employed in its construction were mostly of wood, it being a frame building. Hither the Sultan frequently repaired, for it was his delight to visit this kiosk.

During the Crimean war, this palace was occupied by the British soldiery and used as a hospital. It was henceforth considered polluted, since the Sultan is supposed never to occupy a building after others have used it, much less so after having been used by Christian soldiers who are regarded as giaours (infidels). For this reason Sultan Abdoul Mejid caused it to be torn down, and, in its stead, built a beautiful stone structure, which he never lived to complete. He was succeeded by his brother Abdoul Aziz as Sultan, who carried the work to completion, but who, for some unknown reason, never spent a night within its walls, and although he visited it at times, it is strange to say that these visits were never prolonged above a few minutes upon any occasion. He however built him a summer residence near the city, on its western side, which he frequently visited and spent his time, in company with his wives and officers, in the chase, for he was exceedingly fond of hunting.

6

by very severe earthquakes,* and in the year 260, it was threatened with overthrow by the Goths. It is situated upon beautiful hills which slope down to the water's edge of the gulf of Marmora, about forty-five miles east of the city of Con- stantinople, in Asia Minor, near to Nice, where the great church councils were held. It was not long since rendered famous among Biblical students on account of the discovery of a very old manuscript pertaining to the *teachings of the twelve apostles*.

We learn from church history, and other writings, that this city has passed through some of the most heroic ages of the Christian Church. As early as the year 298, Galerius led a most terrible persecution against the early Christians. At a meeting between two Monarchs, an imperial order was passed causing the splendid church at Nicomedia to be pulled down. After this an edict was issued by the Emperor, ordering all Christian churches to be pulled down, the sacred writings to be destroyed, and the meetings of the Christians were henceforth forbidden. The most terrible modes of punishment and death, which the ingenuity of an

*Under the city of Nicomedia as it now stands, are found many evidences of the ruins of the city in its early days. These consist of ancient buildings, walls iron gates, and numerous other relics, which are all brought to light at different times when excavating for buildings, &c. In digging the foundation for the Greek Monastery which was rebuilt near the city, in the year 1860-61, a great many relics, such as the tombs of the dead, these having sunk into the earth at the time of one of these terrible convulsions of nature. Upon many of these tombs and other stones were found images and ancient writings. Quite a number of them were bought from the Greeks by European antiquarians who carried them to Eu- rope. They also took impressions from the writings of a great many more of these stones, having with them a certain kind of paper prepared for that purpose. The writer's father was an artist, and did much fine painting in this Monastery ; hence it was the writer's privilege to assist his father in this work. He was there- fore an every day witness to these discoveries and very frequently saw these writings copied.

Just out side the city—between it and this same Monastery—is situated the Armenian cemetery which is beautifully overshadowed by stately trees. It is in- closed within a large field, in which may be seen jutting out from the earth, the arched roof of a large ancient Christian church, called Piyur Perotz, that was also sunk by an earthquake. Tradition says that during the terrible persecutions of the early Christians, several thousand persons perished in this church, upon an Easter holiday, whither they had fled for refuge, where they were supposed to be spend- ing their time in prayer and communion service.

evil mind could invent, were, for the purpose, constructed in the city.*

For those many years of incessant persecutions, never before precedented, the brightest evidences of moral heroism and enthusiastic readiness to suffer as martyrs, were given by Christians.

At first heathenism seemed to reign supreme; by it christianity was overrun and persecuted with tortures the most horrible, even to death. But at last the Christians with unsullied faith, confessing their allegiance to Christ with joy and martyrdom, gained a complete victory over heathenism.

For the first time in Nicomedia was published that great fundamental principle of religious liberty, by the edict of Milan, on June 13th, 313, by which a new era was given to the Christian Church, thus according full religious freedom to all. After this, each individual was permitted to worship agreeable to his own belief and faith. Now there arose, all over the Empire, many Christian Churches, the most stately of which was the Church of the Apostles, constructed of marble and other fine building stones. Everywhere could be seen the signs and symbols of the Christian faith. In the city squares the heathen statuary gave place to that of the Christians. There was placed at the entrance to the imperial palace an image of the Good Shepherd, where it could be seen by all who might pass that way. There, also, was to be seen a great picture of Victorious Constantine, represented as holding the *Labarum*, the banner of the cross, having under his feet the great dragon of heathenism, pierced with arrows.

---

*In his boyhood days, the writer frequently visited an old Greek Monastery where the priests took special delight in showing many old paintings representing the horrible instruments of torture and death which were used in the persecutions of the early christians.

8

Still, under Julian of Nicomedia, there appeared a "little cloud," but it passed quickly away. It was but the reaction of expiring heathenism, giving proof that its life was already exhausted. The arrow which pierced the body of Julian, also brought death to ancient heathenism, which as it fell, cried out : "Nazarine, thou hast conquered."

It is sad for Christians to see that Nicomedia, Constantiople, and Nice, together with the surrounding land, so eminently connected with Biblical scenes, as also the Holy land so historically related to the Christian Church, all of which was the very cradle of christianity, should for five centuries be named a Mohammedan country instead of being called a Christian land. Yes, the land in which the apostolic churches were established, and where the Church Fathers fought against paganism, heathenism and heresy, and where many Christians were burned to death, and, as Christian martyrs and heroes, colored that land with their blood for the love of Christ and His holy religion.

To Christians it is indeed a painful matter, but it is not such a strange thing after all. We see that when the Isrealites forsook *God*, He also forsook them—expelled them from their beloved country ; drove them into captivity, and delivered their land to the heathen. We have no doubt but that the *Mohammedan* in that land is but a *rod* in God's hand to smite and punish those corrupted churches. When the Oriental churches in that country began to sink the Church in superstition, and one Christian nation anathe-matized the other, then they, finding a good chance, appeared like swarming locusts, on a mission of destruction to the land which was the cradle of christianity. They soon over-threw the Christian Churches in Africa and oppressed those in Asia, as we learn in Rev. 11-6—"I will come unto you quickly and remove thy candle stick out of his place." But blessed be the name of God, although He "removes" His church, He never destroys it. In due time, He again visits it with his kindness.

While the Oriental Christian nations were deprived of spiritual light and life, and were under bondage and degradation, God, in His great mercy stirred up the *American Christians* to send us their Missionaries to raise them to the glory of their former days. And blessed be that day in which they not only prayed for the coming of the kingdom of God in that land, but also sent us the *gospel* in its simplicity, and some of their best men, whose graves in that country bear witness to their labors for us.

CHAPTER I.

A BRIEF HISTORY OF THE BEGINNING OF THE MISSIONARY
WORK IN NICOMEDIA BY THE AMERICAN BOARD OF
FOREIGN MISSIONS, AND THE GLORIOUS RESULTS
FROM THE SAME.

A little more than fifty years ago missionary visits
to Nicomedia were made by Dr. Wm. Goodell and Rev.
Mr. Dwight, Missionaries sent out by the American Board of
Missions, who brought with them a few copies of the Gospel.
When they came to the city, they stopped at an Armenian
Han (Turkish Hotel) which was kept by a man whose name
was Mom Ju* Aghacy to whom they presented one of these
Gospels. This man observing the pure character and upright
conduct of these good Missionaries, introduced them to his
two friends, Hohannes Nergararian and Murad Varjhabed.
The former of the last two named persons was an aged physician and one of the principal men in the Armenian church in
which he was highly honored and respected ; the latter was a
man who was noted for his learning and scientific research,
being a professor of Science in the great Monastery of Armash
and having there taught many priests and bishops of the
Armenian church, for which reason he had a very great influence over the Armenian nation. He, however, loved the
honor of men rather than the glory of God, but notwith-

*Mom Ju, Turkish for candle seller.

standing this he became the means through whom Simon* of Moosh, a student in the Monastery, received the blessed truths of the gospel and thus became an earnest Christian worker in the cause of Christ. Through the instrumentality of this young student, the following persons were induced to search after the simple truths of the Gospel, viz : Hajy Mel-Kon Karajian, Kit Varjhabed, Baghdosar, Garabed Nergararian,† Megerditch Zaparar, Harutiun Zaparar, and Baron (Mr.) Avedes, a young man who afterwards became one of the first students under Rev. Cyrus Hamlin, D. D., in the Babak Seminary. These young men were wont to retire to the woods, mountains, caves, and other isolated places, where unmolested they might secretly read and search the scriptures and hold prayer meetings.

There were now several American Missionaries in Constantinople, who began to make private visits to these converts from time to time, secretly scattering the precious seed of the Gospel among them and their families, which has since borne so much blessed fruit.

Until now the work was carried on in secret, but God, in His all wise providence, saw fit to provide still other means to carry forward this good work.

*This man is well versed in the ancient or classic Armenian literature, and is a great instrument in advancing the truths of the gospel among his people, and, from that time to the present, is a much honored and beloved minister in a Protestant church in Asia Minor.

†This man was the writer's uncle.

CHAPTER II.

Sultan Abdoul Mejid, being very desirous to awaken within the minds of his people a spirit of industry and improvement, established a woolen factory a few miles from the city. That he might be the more successful in this enterprise, he employed a gentleman from England to superintend the factory. This gentleman was Mr. Beans, who proved to be a true and noble christian man. Mr. Beans rented a large Turkish nobleman's residence situated near the market place. As this gentleman and all his house was under the protection of the English government, all who were disposed to do so, were permitted by him to meet here for worship, and thus be protected from molestation.

At this time it began to be whispered about that a new heresy had appeared among the people. Aghavni,* the Archbishop, hearing this, summoned into his presence Hohannes Nergararian, a sub acolyte, and told him that he had learned that a heresy was among the people, and that he was informed his son Garabed was reported as having become a heretic. The Bishop began to make threats to Nergararian, saying that if he would persuade his son to desist from this strange doctrine, all would be well, but if his son, should persist in that way, he would have to abide the evil consequences that

---

*Aghavni signifies dove.

13

were sure to follow. Nergararian at once forbade his son's attending the meetings of the so called heretics. But in this the father was not successful, for the gospel truth had already taken deep root in the heart of his son.

Seeing that the youth would not yield, they caused him to be bound in chains and thrown into prison for three days and nights with the hope of scaring him into submission, but in vain. He was then banished to the Monastery of Armash as an exile for two years.

In the meantime, Nergararian's other two sons and his married daughters with their husbands became convinced of the Gospel and accepted its divine precepts. When this became known to him, he drove them from under the shelter of his roof, and forbade their return, unless they would renounce their adherence to this faith. This he did not do so much from the zeal which he had for the church, for he was not ignorant of the truth, but he did it that he might retain the honor and respect of men.

During this time Dr. Smith, who was a missionary, and also a physician, visited the city. He was invited to the house of a Protestant brother to preach, but could not make his way there on account of the excited throng which had gathered in the street, his purpose having been made known to them. He, however, succeeded in getting to the house of this brother's sister by passing through a less frequented street. Here he preached to a large and attentive audience. His sermon was a most earnest and impressive one. The words of life which he expounded to them, carried conviction to their hearts, and there was a powerful demonstration of the spirit in the audience. It appeared as if a still small voice had whispered in their ears, "Flee the wrath which is to come

14

and the ceremonial worship of the Church, but strive to follow Christ in spirit and truth, that you may save your souls." Henceforth the light of the Gospel began to dawn in the minds of these people, and they gradually withdrew themselves from their mother church, the *observance* of whose many *rites* and *ceremonies* were supposed to *ensure Heaven* to them.

Some time after this, these brethren were also visited by Rev. B. Schneider whose readiness to preach the Gospel was always "instant in season" and "out of season." He, seeing the inward manifestations of the spirit operating upon the hearts of these converts and their increasing hatred against the superstitions of the church on the one hand, and their persecutions on the other, advised them to use christian forbearance in all things. He further advised them to be prudent, and not to talk about the faults and inconsistencies of the church, but to be steadfast in the faith, and try to shine as christian lights among them. This advice was timely, and the brethren profited much by it.

The people, however, were stirred up and excited to open persecution by the national leaders and heads of the church.

The Priests went from house to house and gathered up all the Protestant books and tracts upon which they could lay their hands and consigned them to the flames. Once five Priests went to the house of Surpuhe* Nergararian and told her that they had heard that both she and her husband had a Testament and were reading it, which act is an unlawful thing for a layman, much more so for a woman to do. "The Patriarch," said they, "has ordered us to collect these books. If you want to know the Scriptures you must listen to the priests in the church. She then answered, "I am surprised !

---

*The writer's mother.

Why should the people be forbidden to read the scriptures, when St. John says, 'I write unto you little children ; I write unto you young men ;' and again 'I write unto you fathers.' And Christ also commands us to search the Scriptures. Besides this, since my husband has read this book, he has become a *temperate* man, *kind* and *indulgent* to his family, but to whom you never before came to advise as to his conduct. But now, since he has been reformed by the reading of this book, *five* of you *long bearded* priests, who heretofore never even inquired into our spiritual condition, now come to advise, and dictate to us what we shall do ; are you therefore not ashamed to ask for it ?" Fearing that her beloved Gospel would be taken from her, she immediately ran up stairs, took her precious book and threw it into the loft of the house, so that they might not find it.

The priests angrily left the house, and after this the people began to publish her and her husband as Protestants. They concluded that if reading the scriptures and practicing its precepts was Protestantism, it must surely be a good thing, for it makes people morally better ; hence that the report branding the Protestants as a bad people must be untrue. In time both she and her husband became identified with the missionary cause. She now not only read the Gospel more zealously, but she began to teach her lady friends and neighbors this Gospel, by reading and preaching to them. Some who before were enemies to these Protestants now became convinced of the truth and also cast their lot with this christian family and others who had already espoused this cause.*

*This lady has for twenty years been connected with the American Board of Foreign Missions as a bible teacher among the native ladies, which position she still honorably fills, being one of the most zealous, earnest and successful workers in this good cause.

CHAPTER III.

The reader's attention will now be directed to Hajy Melkon Karajian for a short time to show the shrewdness with which these native brethren were sometimes obliged to overcome great difficulties.

To this gentleman a box of books was sent by the Missionaries. Learning that it was at the Custom House, he went quite late in the evening—when but few people are accustomed to be in the public places and upon the streets—and brought it to his house. Notwithstanding this precaution, it was reported to some of the principal officers of the church that a box of Protestant books was received by him. These officers at once called a church council as to the matter, in which it was decided that these books must be found and destroyed, and that Karajian should be banished from the city. A sexton who was a secret disciple or friend of these Protestant brethren, and who being present at this council heard this decision, immediately went and informed him of their purpose, thus putting him upon his guard. Karajian forthwith called a Protestant brother named Hagop Beghadosian, who was a gardener, to aid him in concealing the books. It is the custom of these gardeners to carry their manure in panniers placed upon the back of a mule or horse to their gardens. The gardener took the books and put them in the bottom of his panniers, and plac-

17

ing a cloth upon them, covered them with manure. Having thus concealed them, he conveyed them to his garden where they were secreted in a place of safety. Scarcely had the books been removed when the priests came, accompanied by a number of the church officials and police, followed by an excited mob, to search for the books. The search, as a matter of course, proved a fruitless one. The mob, seeing their design frustrated, became furious with rage, but since nothing could be effected or proven they were obliged to return without molesting or harming any one.

A portion of these books were distributed among the people of the city, and the remainder were sent to an Armenian gentleman named Kavalgian, in the city of Ada-Pazar, about eighteen miles east of Nicomedia. By these means the Gospel fire was enkindled in the hearts of the people all over these cities.

When the priests and national leaders saw that, in spite of their efforts to suppress this missionary movement, these religious books and tracts were being scattered abroad in the nation, and that many of them had already embraced this new doctrine, they began a most violent persecution. One evening, at a very unusual time, the people were summoned to church by the church crier, who heralded abroad the news that a special order had been received from the Patriarch. After a great concourse of people had assembled together, one of the priests read the patriarch's order and urged them to resist this new doctrine with might and main, and harangued them to open persecution and violence.

The next day the Armenian representatives were summoned from the neighboring towns and villages and organized into a General Council. On the outside of the building,

18

in through the entrance, on both sides of the walk, the city roughs and rabble were stationed with club-like weapons in their hands. The Protestants were then summoned to appear before this General Council. The Bishop examined each one of these individually, demanding of him whether he would henceforth obey the behests of the Council, or abide the evil consequences which were sure to follow.

When Zeparar Megerditch was brought before this august personage, he bravely answered that it was his purpose to stand firm in his faith and maintain the truth, notwithstanding their threats, and ended by quoting the language of Peter and John, "Whether it be right in the sight of God, to hearken unto you more than to God, judge ye." One of the chief men in the council said: "Baron Megerditch, I have read and studied both the Psalms and the Acts of the Apostles, do you therefore presume to teach us the scriptures?" This was intended as a rebuke. There was a wealthy gardener in the Council, who, seeing the readiness with which Megerditch quoted the scriptures, (he being only a common plasterer as his trade name indicates,) said to him, "When did *you* become so learned?" He replied, "When *you* were planting your *egg plants*, I was reading and studying the Bible."

Harutiun Zeparar was next called. The Bishop asked him, "Have you not greatly dishonored your father-in-law* by following after this heresy?" He answered, "I *greatly dishonored* him when I sought pleasure in the public wine houses. I was as a lost sheep, but none came to seek me, for the shepherd of the flock was an hireling. But I have found the true Shepherd and Bishop of my soul who gave His life for me."

*Hohannes Nergararian.

19

Thus, one by one, all were brought before the Council and examined.

A very influential Armenian, named Kevork Aga, said, in the course of making some remarks before this Council, "I have an only son whom I would rather follow to his grave than see Protestantism go on unmolested, without making an effort on my part in helping to root it out from our midst." In a few days his son was no more numbered with the living. How easily an over-ruling Providence can thwart the evil purposes of men !

In this Council they were at a loss to know how they might be able to subdue this influence which had already become a power among the people of the nation. They finally decided to send the priests and deacons to the wives and families of those persons who had espoused the Protestant faith. These, by using arguments and threats, were, if possible, to turn the influence of wife and children against the husband, thus fulfilling the words of Christ as we see by reading Math. 10 : 35, which says, "For I come to set a man at variance against his father, and the daughter against her mother, and the daughter-in-law against her mother-in-law."

The Council also drew up a confession of faith setting forth the doctrines of the church. Thus all who were suspected of Protestantism, were asked to acknowledge by affixing thereto their signature. Those who would refuse to do so were to be anathematized and expelled from the church, and more than this, they were to be deprived from having communications and dealings with their fellow men. This confession read as follows :

"Do you believe there is one triune God, the Father, Son, and Holy Ghost, these three in one?

"Do you believe that in the Holy Communion, the bread and wine become the real flesh and blood of Christ?

"Do you believe that the Saints who have died are mediators between God and man?

"Do you believe that the crucifix, annointed with holy oil, and the bones of Saints, are proper objects of worship and reverence, and that it is lawful to make pilgrimages to Jerusalem to see the sepulchre of Christ and of the Saints?

"Do you believe that the Priests as Christ's representatives, can do sacrifice for us, and that through prayer, they have the power to forgive our sins; also that they can pray for the benefit and deliverance of the departed spirits (dead men's souls)?" Etc.

The Protestants were now compelled to accept this confession of faith, or to reject it and abide by whatever might follow.

The acts of this council stirred up the Missionaries to renewed diligence, and they began to visit the people more frequently than ever.

As soon as Rev. Mr. Dwight and Dr. Goodel were informed of the Council's proceedings, they advised the brethren not to separate themselves from the Armenian communion, saying that, if they did so, the work would not advance so rapidly.

This was also advised by Dr. Smith. He illustrated this matter to them by saying that if they wished to burn the timber from off a mountain, they would not set fire to it at but one, but at many places, and in this way the object desired would soon be accomplished.

But to remain in the church they were obliged to accept the confession of faith drawn up by the Council. The Missionaries did not mean they should accept a thing which was so unscriptural and against the dictates of their consciences, yet in giving this advise, they showed great wisdom. First, they did not take upon themselves the responsibility of causing a separation in the church and nation ; secondly, they gave these Protestant brethren an opportunity to learn from their own experience that it was impossible for them to remain in the church.

Nevertheless the most honored and influential of the older brethren placed themselves in the bosom of the nation. This, however, many who were younger in years and less experienced, refused to do. The former became more highly honored and respected than ever, but the latter were more bitterly persecuted. Among the former number were Hajy Melkon Karajian and Garabed Karagoesian. So well had these two brethren ingratiated themselves into the good graces of the churchmen that they were appointed the superintendents over the schools in the church.

Der* Harutiun, a highly honored priest who was also a secret disciple, opened a female school, supported by the missionaries, a fact, however, unknown to the people. To this school the people were urged, by the superintendents (Karajian and Karagoesian), to send their daughters.

Those who were less prudent were anathematized and turned out from their houses and families, and even from their places of business. They were caught in the streets, beaten with heavy clubs, and spit upon. The people were strictly forbidden to have any dealings with them, and no one was allowed to give them a morsel of bread or even a cup of water, under penalty of like treatment. Thus

---

*Der signifies Lord or Master, and is usually prefixed to the name of a priest.

22

they were outlawed and placed at the mercy of the public.

Many thus driven out of society, not being permitted to carry on their legitimate occupations, were obliged to sell and sacrifice their properties, so that they might obtain means to live ; many ladies were necessitated to part with their jewelry and ornaments, to obtain bread for themselves and their children.

Some of these persecuted and distressed persons were kindly and nobly assisted and sheltered by the Missionaries and Mr. Beans. These kind friends with loving hearts and willing hands gave liberally of their means to gladden the hearts of these poor downtrodden and despised Christians.

CHAPTER IV.

Although severely persecuted themselves, they also showed great dissatisfaction against those brethren who did not bravely stand up for the truth. They began to chide them and to prick their conscience, and insinuated that they were seeking worldly honors and esteem, saying that they were like unto Demas, of whom Paul writes, "For Demas has forsaken me, having loved the present world."

By this time Hohannes Nergararian, whose son Garabed had been exiled to the Monastery of Armash, had also secretly become Protestant at heart. Garabed now returned home from the Monastery, but his father was still unwilling to receive him. Although his conscience smote him, and he was halting between two opinions, he preferred the honor which was bestowed upon him by the heads of the church.

Nergararian's house was beautifully located upon one of the principal streets of the city just opposite of which was a very large old Turkish cemetery.

Garabed being refused admittance into his parental home, made it his custom for a time to go into this cemetery, where he would stand upon a grave stone and thus address his father :—

"O father, why have you cast me out from home ? Were your requests not in opposition to the holy scriptures and my conscience, I would most gladly obey. I have *no desire* to disobey your behests, but Christ says, 'He that loveth father or mother more than Me is not worthy of Me.' Remember that for the truth's sake the father shall be against the child, 'and the children shall rise up against their parents.' 'And ye shall be hated of all men for my name's sake.' Father, I pity you. You are not doing this against me, but against Christ and His Holy word. Think of it, father, I am sure you will acknowledge the wrong in time to come. You will then know that I was in the right. I pity you, father. Don't do it, father. Don't do it. I pity you. Think of your soul."

Delivering his odd sermon from the grave stone from time to time and being dressed in a monkish garb, he at first presented quite a ludicrous appearance to his parents and family, but the truth of his remarks so strangely delivered, caused restlessness in the heart of his father, and natural parental love melted his mother to tears. She therefore urged her husband to receive their son back to their home and hearts.

Nergararian and others, who together with him up to this time had believed that much more good could be accomplished by remaining in the church, and that by so doing, a reform could be brought about, now saw from their past experience that such a course only tended to lessen their christian zeal, and that it was only hiding their light under a bushel. They therefore held a council in which it was decided that Nergararian should go and confess the whole matter to Aghavni the Bishop. This he at once did, telling the Bishop that hitherto he had been practicing hypocrisy and concealed the truth for his sake and the honors of men. He told him that his consciousness of right and justice would no longer permit him to accept the dogmas of the church, and that henceforth he would receive back his son Garabed, let the consequence be what it might.

When the Bishop heard this very unexpected declaration, he was greatly surprised and troubled. He exclaimed, "O Nergararian, should you do this, how can I suppress this growing dissatisfaction among the people? You are regarded, by them, as a father, hence your example will have a bad effect. Truth is like the sun whose light cannot be hid; but now the days are evil. The people are ignorant, and while they are very conscientious and strict in the observances of the ceremonial law of the church, they think it no great matter to persecute those who oppose their religion. Read the history of the saints and learn what horrible deeds were wrought in their day. I am aged and can not endure the persecutions which would be sure to follow, were I to oppose the wishes of the nation. I have no other course to pursue than to obey and carry out the mandates of the Patriarch. Should that not be agreeable to your wishes, do not censure me. Again I say, wait, do not act too rashly; it is not yet the time to decide so grave a matter."

Nergararian answered, "We can wait for time, but time does not wait for us." Saying this, he departed.

After this interview with Aghavni, he at once received to his home his son and all the remainder of his children who had been driven away. One Sunday morning, soon after this, his wife was not permitted to enter the church because they had received back their anathematized son.

Nergararian now opened his house for Sunday services, and all who had espoused the Protestant cause—both those who had left the church, and those who still remained in it—came here to worship, and formed one congregation.

Der Harutiun, the priest of whom mention has already been made, after performing the religious ceremonies in his own church, would secretly come and take part in these services. The missionaries were also present at these meetings from time to time.

From day to day persecutions now began to increase. Upon the Easter morning following the events just related, an immensely large number of people were assembled in the church. The holy altar was closed from the view of the audience by a drawn curtain as a sign of mourning. The Bishop arose and, in tears, thus addressed the people :—

"O blessed congregation, I have indeed sad news to tell you this morning. Acolyte Nergararian has received back into his house his anathematized son and children. Before he was called Boyaji Baba (Father Nergararian) and a pillar of church, but now he is become a heretic and is spiritually dead ; therefore to him and his house be, *Anathema Maranatha*, and let those who hear say, *amen*." The congregation arose and, turning their faces away from the altar and the image of the Virgin Mary, cried out with a mighty voice, "AMEN!" After the Bishop had paused a moment as if to give his words a greater emphasis, he again repeated the solemn curse and added, "*He is spiritually dead.* As we can not have any intercourse with the dead, so neither can we have any communication or dealings with such as are anathematized ; therefore whosoever hath communication, dealing, or business with him or his household, let such an one also be *Anathema Maranatha*, and let all who hear say, Amen." Again came the response, "*Amen!*"

This last response was mingled with many sighs and tears—some weeping because of their kinship, others, because of the love and esteem which they had for Nergararian and his family.

The people now became wild with excitement. A general persecution was instituted against the so called heretics. They at once closed Nergararian's place of business. His house was stoned, the windows broken, and the doors bedaubed and defaced. The Protestants throughout the entire city were mobbed and assailed ; their houses were stoned ; their windows broken and smashed into pieces. Even the very tiles upon the house tops were knocked off and broken up. Stones were hurled at their houses and shops like showers of hail.

While this was going on, twelve ruffians who had become somewhat intoxicated with wine, secretly took counsel together in a wine house to kill Nergararian, thinking that this could easily be accomplished without detection on account of the tumult. But the plot was overheard by an Armenian teacher whose house was next to Nergararian's. Going to Nergararian's window, he quietly informed him of his danger, and advised him to be on his guard. He at once shut himself up in his house where he and his family quietly remained for several days until the excitement was allayed.

A brother, named Hajy Sarkis, during the excitement of this day, was driven away from his home by his wife and his mother-in-law, without even being permitted to look upon his own children. He now endured very many hardships, being compelled to struggle, as best he could, to keep himself above want. At last he took sick in a Turkish Han, but not even a Protestant brother was permitted to administer to his wants. He was, however, frequently visited by many influential Armenians who tried to persuade him to desist from the step which he had taken, but his only answer was, "Who shall separate me from the love of Christ?" "Do you not wish to see your children?" was asked of him. He replied, "Oh, that I would, but not permitted : Oh, could I but see my Savior!"

A priest named Thadeus, who was his confessor, having a special regard for him, went to the Bishop and obtained permission to take him to his own house, giving the assurance that he would be able to win him back to the church. He accordingly had him brought to his home. But it was soon found that he was already fast approaching the hour of his dissolution. According to the teachings of the Armenian church, if any one dies without receiving absolution for sin and the holy communion, he cannot be buried in an Armenian cemetery. For this reason Thadeus tried to persuade him to be absolved and to commune. This Hajy Sarkis refused, in as much as he could not accept the doctrine of transubstantiation for his atonement and the remission of sin. Said he, "I have already communed with Christ." Soon after this he died.

Thadeus being unwilling to acknowledge his inability to reclaim him, concealed the fact that Hajy Sarkis had died without receiving absolution and the holy communion. He was therefore buried in the cemetery.

After burial services, it is customary to sit in little groups in the cemetery, under the shade trees, to eat simit (a pretzel like cake) and drink rakee (whiskey), thus driving away grief by social enjoyment. Upon this occasion, it so happened that a Protestant brother was among the people, though this fact was not observed at the time. Thadeus, the priest, was conversing with a group of persons concerning the heretics. A member of very high standing accidentally remarked to Thadeus, "You priests are much to blame for this heresy."

29

Thadeus thinking that his deception had in some way been made known to him, angrily replied : "You must not censure me too harshly. You should not urge me to the whole truth. I did all in my power, but *could* not persuade him to commune, the *accursed* man ! He told me he had already communed with Christ." Just at this very interesting point of the conversation, Harutiun Zaparar, the brother referred to, was observed, and they at once became silent upon that subject, but he had already heard the very important declaration that Hajy Sarkis had not communed, but died a Protestant.

This incident gave rise to many grave thoughts in the minds of these brethren ; for while they did not believe the doctrine of transubstantiation, but that the holy communion was needful as an act commemorative of the dying love of the blessed Savior, yet they were ignorant as to its administration.

Another matter of no little importance to them, was the privation of burial in the Armenian cemeteries, or even in any other, since they could not do so without being communicants ; hence they were left without a place of burial—one reason why they so patiently bore their persecutions.

CHAPTER V.

Concerning the communion, there was much discussion, and the brethren began to make inquiries of the Missionaries as to the manner in which it should be administered. In answering their inquiries the Missionaries were very careful, since they were as yet mere babes in spiritual things, and had to be fed with "the sincere milk of the word ;" for these converts had been accustomed from their youth to see this solemn service celebrated with much ceremony, since the Armenians perform it with greater pomp than even that of the Catholics. They were therefore instructed to read and meditate upon suitable passages from the New Testament Scriptures having reference to the subject, especially that of the Lord's last supper with His disciples just before His crucifixion, so that they might better understand its significance and importance. In time, after they had become conversant with our Savior's command and teachings at His last supper, they felt a very great desire for the holy communion, being impressed with its importance as a means of grace, and resolved to embrace the earliest opportunity to celebrate this Holy ordinance ; hence, when the next Missionary, Dr. Wood, visited them, they asked him to administer it to them.

Pursuant to their wishes, Dr. Wood appointed a meeting in the house of Mr. Beans. Upon this occasion quite a number of persons—two of which were females—presented themselves as candidates for this Holy service. Upon examination they gave bright evidence of their acceptance with Christ, and received their first communion. A little girl (an infant) was baptized upon this occasion, it being the first Protestant baptism administered in Nicomedia.

Here then in the house of Mr. Beans, through Rev. Dr. Wood, was established the second organized church in Turkey, July 20, 1846, the first organization having been established at Pera, Constantinople, about two weeks previous. Soon after this followed organizations at Ada-Pazar and Trabuzan, and at many other places.

CHAPTER VI.

With the establishment of these organizations came persecutions still more bitter and severe than before. At this time a demand was made upon the Armenian nation; by the Turkish government, for a certain number of men to serve in the army. ● When such demands were made, the principal men of the nation usually met in council, and there secretly determined who should be sent to serve under the Sultan. Such persons were generally drafted from the lower classes, and after a list of the names of such as should go, was made out, it was at once handed to the Kachya, or tax collector, whose duty was not only to collect the national tribute money, but also to attend to whatever business the nation might have with the government. The nation, whose hatred knew no bounds against this little devoted band of Protestant Christians, saw at once their opportunity of wreaking their vengeance upon it; they therefore made up their quota of men from these brethren.

As an eagle pounces upon its prey, so the officials seized Garabed Nergararian and threw him into the common prison. His parents and friends divining their purpose, namely that of sending him away to serve in the army, used every means in their power to secure his release, but in vain. The next morning he was taken from the prison, and, between two sol-

33

diers with drawn swords, he was hastened to the vessel awaiting his transportation. In tears he besought his guards to permit him once more to look upon the face of his aged mother and to give her his final farewell, but all to no purpose. It only seemed to increase their cruelty, and they forced him along more rapidly at the points of their swords. His mother was as yet awaiting his release, but when the sad news of his misfortune was broken to her, she was immediately stricken down with palsy from which she never recovered.

Soon after this, two other brethren, named Baghdoser and Stephen, were also unexpectedly conscripted and sent to the barracks of Sellemia.

It became apparent that the heads of the church had determined to rid the city of the Protestants by conscripting them into the Turkish soldiery—a most dreaded calamity indeed. Hence, no sooner is the smoke of the government steamer seen heading its course toward the city than they flee into the mountains or Mr. Bean's factory,* in order to escape what to them would be even worse than penitentiary.

---

*We read in Genesis 19 : 1, 2 and 3,—"And there came two angels to Sodom at even ; and Lot sat in the gate of Sodom ; and Lot, seeing them . . . said, . . . turn in, I pray you, into your servant's house, and tarry all night. And they said, NAY, but we will abide in the street all night. And he PRESSED them greatly ; and they turned in unto him, and entered into his house : &c."
Now it was the sole purpose of the angels from the first, to lodge with Lot that night, but according to the custom of the country it would have been very rude or impolite of them to have accepted his first invitation, hence they permitted him to press his invitation before they could accept it with propriety. Strange to say, this custom still prevails to-day in Asiatic Turkey, hence an invitation even to a meal is never accepted until the party so invited has been repeatedly urged to do so.
Two of the brethren who had one day taken refuge at the factory of Mr. Beans during one of their flights, were, by that gentleman, kindly invited to sit up to the table and take tea with the family. As a matter of course, according to this Oriental custom, they refused. But Mr. Beans, being an Englishman whose custom was entirely different, did not repeat the invitation, and they were permitted to pass through the night upon an empty stomach, which was by no means a very pleasant situation, since they were very tired and hungry, having walked some distance. The next morning, when Mr. Beans asked them whether they were hungry and invited them to breakfast, they eagerly answered, "Yes! Yes!!" During the twenty-four hours of hunger which they had just passed through, they learned that it was not always safe to be governed by a mock modesty, and that it was often well to take a man at his word.

34

It was, however, impossible for them to remain in the mountains, for during the rigor of winter, no shelter could there be found, hence some other means of escape was necessary.

In the mean time they were informed that some unknown friend had bribed the Kachya, who being eager for gain, willingly permitted those to escape, whom he and the Turkish police might be seeking. When these officers came in contact with any one whose name was upon the list of conscripts, he would at once be notified of their purpose by a certain sign previously agreed upon, and the party sought, would immediately seek refuge in the house of Mr. Beans. This they could very easily do, since they were unknown to the police.

Nevertheless, while they were thus permitted to escape, they felt many compunctions of conscience on account of the three brethren who had already been sent away; for they now heard many sorrowful things concerning their condition. In a letter which had recently been received from one of these unfortunate brethren, were written these words:

"O brethren, we beseech you, pray for us. Our trials are indeed severe; our difficulties and perils are many. Yet all these are endurable except one thing needful. Oh, that we could, like Nathaniel, find a fig tree under which to pray in secret, and there hold sweet communion with our Lord! But in our room, we cannot enjoy such a blessed privilege, for in each room there are no less than six or eight Turkish soldiers whose blasphemy and corrupt conversation is ever sounding in our ears, and who, when they see a Bible in our hands, immediately club us over our heads with the stocks of their guns."

35

When the Missionaries heard this letter read, their hearts were greatly touched, and at once set about devising some plan to secure their release. After these brethren had been in the army for about two years, the Missionaries succeeded in their purpose by hiring substitutes to take their place; and thus they were once more permitted to return to their homes and friends.

The native brethren seeing the wonderful love and sympathy exhibited towards these unfortunates ones by the Missionaries, were constrained to love and esteem them as their fathers, and for this reason, they became more greatly encouraged than ever, and grew stronger in the faith.

To show how the kindness of these good Missionaries was appreciated, it is but necessary to relate one little incident which is as follows: A poor brother, who together with his wife, was cast out from home, seeing such a great display of Christian love and sympathy manifested by the Missionaries, sold a portion of his cooking utensils so that he could make a feast for them, and in this way express his thankfulness in behalf of his persecuted brethren; although the sacrifice which this poor brother made, was never known to them.

CHAPTER VII.

According to the custom of the Armenian church, after the priest has sacrificed the emblems of the holy communion he holds the chalice up before the congregation saying, as he extends it toward heaven, "This is the life, the hope, and the atonement for the remission of sin." This, Der Harutiun felt he could not do, it being in direct opposition to his conscience ; hence, when he celebrated this service, he substituted the word *that* (Armenian, na) for *this* (sa) in presenting the chalice to the congregation, meaning that not the *emblems*, but that Christ Himself was *the life, the hope, and the atonement* for the remission of sin.

Upon a certain Sunday, after celebrating these services, he came as usual to the meeting of the brethren. Some one called his attention to the fact that he had substituted the word *that* for *this* in his morning service, when he held up the chalice before the congregation, remarking at the same time, "In this you are not understood. You ought openly manifest the truth to the people." He replied, "I am not situated as you are. They have invested me with priestly orders. Nevertheless this shall be my last celebration of Mass. Therefore pray for me."

Upon the next Sabbath morning, the gochnocs* were beaten longer than usual, and the Zhamgotches† were sent forth to summon the people to church. Soon an immense audience was assembled and everything indicated that something unusual was to take place. Der Harutiun was present, and upon him all eyes were turned with eager expectation, for it was now known that he had recanted the doctrines of the church. The Bishop arose and pointing to Harutiun thus addressed the congregation :—

"O blessed people, among the priests this man was indeed very prominent, and was worthy to be called Der Harutiun and father. But he has become a heretic and is therefore *Chik Harutiun.*" The last two words were several times repeated so as to give them a still greater emphasis, meaning that Harutiun was now spiritually dead and had become as nothing to the church.

Harutiun was divested of his sacerdotal robes from his miter to his slippers, dragged down from the altar, and given to the people to do with him as they pleased, the Bishop meanwhile pronouncing the solemn curse, "Let him be anathema maranatha." He also repeated the words, "*Chik Harutiun, chik Harutiun.*" To these last words Harutiun answered, "Gah harutiun! gah harutiun!‡ (There is a resurrection, there is a resurrection.) Then God will reward every man according to his work."

---

*At the time spoken of, the Mohammedans did not allow a bell to be used in their country, hence other means were employed to summon the people to church. For this purpose the gochnoc was used. This was nothing more or less than a board and a piece of steel, each of which was suspended from a pole and beaten with hammers.

†A person whose duty it was to go out upon the street corners to call the people to church.

‡Harutiun signifies the resurrection, and Chik, nothing. In ancient Armenian it refers to the doctrine of the Sodducees, who taught that there was no resurrection. The Bishop simply meant that Harutiun was no more regarded by them as a Priest, but as nothing at all. Harutiun, however, referred to the resurrection—a play upon the words comprising his own name.

38

He was now seized by the people, beaten, kicked, and spit upon. They carried him to the Khootz—a building occupied by the Bishops and vartabeds—and employed a person who was a most bitter enemy to the Protestants, to shave off his beard. In doing this, he cut and hacked his face in a most shameful manner, so that the blood ran down his cheeks. He was then thrust out upon the street and ignominiously marched in front of the people. His beard was tied to the top of a pole and carried in front of the procession as an ensign. As they marched him along, they beat and kicked him, crying all the while, "Chik Harutiun, Chik Harutiun." The priestly office with which he was vested with so much pomp and ceremony, they took from him in the most disgraceful manner possible.

Having been thus shamefully maltreated, he was set at liberty. He remained concealed at home until his face was healed and his beard grew long enough to hide the scars of his face, for among the Orientals it is a disgrace to have the beard shaven, especially that of a priest.

Being thus entirely freed from the nominal church, he wholly consecrated himself to the work so earnestly begun.

Whenever he was seen upon the street, he was mocked and jeered by the people. Even the boys hooted and shouted at him, and in this way his presence was heralded to the city whenever he was seen upon the public thoroughfares.

Indeed the rabble and the low class of people made it their business to stone the Protestant houses every evening for a time. But notwithstanding these bitter persecutions, the gospel work was moving on more rapidly and pleasantly than ever.

There was another Priest named Der Vertanes who was

very intelligent, and highly honored by the people. He too, like Harutiun, had become Protestant at heart, and entertained like views. Of this, he also was suspected. Seeing the treatment which Harutiun received at their hands, and being apprised of their suspicions, he fled to Constantinople and rented a house in Pera. The Patriarch of the city several times sent his Kachya to summon Vertanes into his presence, but Vertanes surmising his purpose, always found an excuse to prevent his accompanying the Kachya thither. The Patriarch again sent for him and demanded his immediate presence. Seeing the Patriarch's messengers at the door, Vertanes, having a razor at hand for the purpose, went to the window, and leaning out of it, he took his razor and cut off a portion of his beard saying as he did so, "I know what the Patriarch wishes ; here, take this to him." Seeing that their designs were frustrated by Vertanes' shrewdness, they left, and he was never troubled again. But he was anathematized as a devil and destroyer of the church.

CHAPTER VIII.

In the meantime the Armenian leaders brought an accusation against H. Nergararian before the Turkish government, charging him with trying to urge the people to rebellion with the intent of becoming subjects to the English rule. The Kachya together with the police, was sent to arrest him and bring him before the Turkish Court, where they thought to have him condemned and sent away into exile.

No sooner had he learned that the officers were at his door than he hastily called his family around him and prayed for God's protection over all his house. Commending them to the care of a kind and overruling Providence, he went with them to the court house, where were assembled his accusers, the Turkish Council; and the Bishop and Priests of the church.

But God in His infinite wisdom ever watches over those who strive to love and serve Him, and in Whom they put their sole trust and confidence.

As soon as he entered the Court, the Pasha seeing him, commanded that a chair be brought for him, for he was the Pasha's physician, and by him he was very highly respected not only on account of his eminence as a physician, but also for his noble character. Nergararian declining the proffered chair, said, "Most gracious Effendim, I am not worthy to be seated in the presence of this august body (pointing to the

Armenian representatives), but I pray you, that your majesty may be kind enough to inform me as to the purpose of my being summoned before this Court." The Pasha knowing full well that Nergararian would never be guilty of such an accusation, angrily addressing himself to those representatives said, "Is *this* the man, this aged father, whom you accuse before me?" His accusers remaining silent, the Pasha again repeated the question. Still receiving no answer, he turned to Nergararian and asked, "Is it true that you have been stirring up many of the people to rebellion for the purpose of becoming English subjects?" "Pasha, Effendim," answered Nergararian, "I will account myself happy indeed, should you permit me an opportunity to give a simple explanation of this matter." The Pasha commanded him to speak on. He then presented his defense in these words: "Pasha Effendim, I am quite an aged man as you see, and have spent the greater part of my life in the church, adhering strictly to all its rites and ceremonies and keeping all the fasts and feasts. For a number of years I held the office of an acolyte. During the time that I served the church in this capacity, did I but take the Bible in my hand, the Priest would at once say 'Put it down, put it down. It is unlawful for a layman to read this holy book; for such a sacred thing, you are too unworthy; only Priest and collegians are permitted to read it.' Hence I was very ignorant as to its teachings; but blessed be God, nations from a distant land, of a different speech and different religion, were stirred up to send us the gospel in its simplicity. And may God add many thousand days to the Sultan's life that he opened the doors of his country to His Holy Word. Effendim, when I read in this Holy book, the commandment which says, 'Thou shalt not make unto thee any graven image, or likeness or anything, . . . Thou shalt not bow down thyself to them, nor serve them; for I the Lord thy God am a jealous God.' Effendim, these words caused me great trouble and anxiety of mind; for I have not only bowed myself down before images and pictures,* and burnt wax candles and offered incense before them, but in tears I even *kissed* those pictures and implored their aid. In so doing, have I not *greviously sinned* in the sight of God? Effendim, I leave my cause to your judgment. Whom shall I obey, God or man? Which should I most fear, God's just judgment, or man's threatenings?"

When the Pasha heard these words, he burned with indignation, and turning to the Armenian prelates he said, "Is this then the grave offense of this aged man? Your report is of a very different character—a mere pretence; a *false* accusation. Away you *pulparestlar* (idolators)! Begone from my sight! Henceforth, if I hear any more such false accusations or tumult, it shall not be well with you. You shall abide the consequences,"

Nergararian's accusers being only too glad to drop the matter, immediately left the court room, and from this time on, the Bishop never ventured even to anathematize another member. He advised all henceforth to let these people alone. But by his former acts of intolerance, his influence over the people in a great degree was lost, and they were no more willing to regard his admonitions, for his previous example had been a bad one.

---

*All kinds of images and pictures are so obnoxious and hateful to Mohammedans that even a pictured cigarette paper or match box are destroyed by them, and to them a handkerchief with a picture upon it, cannot be sold. They look upon the so-called Christians as idolators. In this particular, the Turks have much greater respect for the Protestants, since they also oppose the worship of images; hence they aided in protecting the Protestants against the persecutions of the nominal christians.

43

The Pasha kindly addressing himself to Nergararian advised him to return quietly and peacefully to his home. Before leaving the court, he returned many sincere thanks to the Pasha for what had been done for him, and requested that he might be permitted to hold a special meeting in his house the following evening, for the purpose of asking God's blessings and protaction upon the Sultan's life and the lives of all his officers. This request the Pasha most cheerfully granted.

Nergararian at once notified the brethren of his purpose. In God's providence it so happened that Absalom, the first ordained native pastor, at Pera, Constantinople, came to Nicomedia that day and preached at Nergararian's house that evening. During the services a brother came into the house, went to Nergararian, and whispered something in his ear. He at once arose and went out, and, to his utter astonishment, he saw that his house was surrounded by Turkish guards who were sent there by order of the Pasha, for the purpose of protecting them from any disturbance on the part of the people. He returned many thanks to the captain of the guards. The captain kindly told him that they were sent by order of the Pasha.

When this fact was made known to Rev. Absalom, he immediately changed his discourse from the Armenian to the Turkish language and in it conducted the service to the end. He spoke loud and distinctly, so that he could be understood by the guards on the outside, and especially invoked the blessings of God upon the Sultan, the Pasha, and all their officers. The guard hearing this, told it to the Pasha who was greatly pleased, and after this he always showed a readiness to grant whatever might be asked of him.

CHAPTER IX.

A short time after the event related above, services were being held preparatory to a communion season, at which time several more persons were examined and received into membership. During these services news was received that a brother named Azaryan Garabed was dying and wished some of the brethren to come and pray with him. Rev. Absalom in company with several others went at once to encourage him and to commend him to God. After they had prayed with him, he said, "To-morrow I will spend my first Sabbath in the heavenly kingdom, but my body will cause you trouble, since you have no place of burial in which to lay it," "Give yourself no anxiety of mind about this," said they, "God will provide a place where your body can rest in peace." Asking the blessings of God upon him, they bid him a last farewell and departed.

During the evening services the house was crowded. A giant like man named Matig,* who was a leader among the

*This man was among the rabble at the time when the first Council was held and in which were presented the articles of faith previously spoken of. Matig, it seems, had stationed himself just at the entrance of the room in which this council was held, having in his hand a large club for the purpose of beating those who might refuse to sign this paper. A certain brother named Saprich Megerditch, seeing Matig with his club, was, for this reason, induced to sign the articles of faith. Afterward, feeling a great distress of conscience about the matter, he went to the Bishop and demanded that his name be erased from the paper. When he was asked why he signed it, he replied, "I was afraid of Matig's club,"

city roughs, came with a number of his companions, to the house, for the purpose of creating a disturbance. It was so arranged that he himself should go up into the room where the meeting was in progress while they remained outside. At a certain signal previously agreed upon, they were to enter, rush upon the people, cause a general confusion and uproar, and then escape. It being the communion service, the minister with tears coursing down his cheeks, was preaching most earnestly upon the sufferings and crucifixion of our Savior. Matig began to feel the power of his words and from him escaped many long and deep sighs. He now had not only forgotten his purpose, but also his companions who by this time were growing impatient, and began to throw small pebbles against the windows and cry "Matig, Matig." Hearing this he angrily ran down stairs and told them that he would at once stab to death with his own knife, the first one who dared make any disturbance whatever. It is needless to say there was no further trouble upon this occasion. Matig came back and manifested a great interest in the services.

Thus by softening the lion heart of this man, God frustrated their evil designs and permitted His people to hold their worship in peace.

CHAPTER X.

After the service was ended, the news came that the sick brother was dead.

The heart of his mother was not only made heavy and sad on account of the loss of her dear son, but she was much troubled because she knew not where to lay his body that it might rest in peace. Some of the brethren at once went to comfort her, and to make arrangement for his burial. They strictly cautioned her not to make his death known to the public until they should perfect the arrangements for his funeral.

A man who owned a vineyard just opposite the Armenian Cemetery, was prevailed upon to sell it for a like use, but before it could be used as a cemetery, it was necessary to obtain a permit from the government.

These brethren remained in council all that night trying to devise some plan by which they might accomplish their design. They finally concluded to lay the matter before the Pasha.

The next day Hohannes Nergararian, taking with him Hajy Melkon and several others, went to the Pasha and presenting to him the object of their errand thus addressed him "Effendim, be it known unto you that not long ago, one of our number* was called from our midst by death, and it was with much difficulty that we could obtain a place to lay him away to rest. O Effendim, we beseech you to grant us a permit to buy a piece of ground upon which to bury our dead. And should you be pleased to grant this our request, we vouchsafe great honor and glory to you, and to us it will indeed be an exceedingly great favor." The Pasha then inquired as to whether they had in view any suitable place which they might be able to secure. Pointing to Kooyumjy Harutiun, Nergararian answered, "This man is willing to sell us his vineyard for that purpose, if permitted." "Is it so?" inquired the Pasha. Harutiun replied, "If your Gracious Highness so will."

The Pasha then granted them the desired permit stamped with his own seal. To the Pasha they returned many thanks for his kind and courteous considerations, and made known to him the fact that one of their number was now lying a corpse at his home. When the Pasha learned this, he immediately commanded the captain of the guards to take a number of men and go with them so that they might be protected from molestation during the funeral services.

By this time it became known that a Protestant funeral was to take place. Soon the streets were filled with people. Many stood in the doorways, windows, and other recesses, to see the funeral cortege.

The body was brought out of the house and the guards which the Pasha had sent, took their place in front of the pro-

---

*The case referred to was that of a little son of an anathematized brother whose name was Kemahl. This little boy died some time previous to this event. The father went to the Priests to obtain their permission to bury his little child in the Armenian cemetery, but they refused to grant it. Two of the brethren then took the child's body and quietly attempted to bury it in the cemetery, but failed in their purpose. They then made an effort to bury it in a private garden, but even this was not allowed. Thus they were driven from place to place until finally they were compelled to bury it secretly near the bank of a river. They did not even dare to mark his little grave from fear of discovery.

cession, but the way was closed up by a clamorous and excited mob who began to hoot and yell at the procession, making a hideous uproar with their oaths and indecent language. Notwithstanding the presence of the guards who with their scourges, were trying to make way to pass through the throng, they threw stones at the Protestants and even spit upon them. While the guards were trying to force the people aside, an Armenian woman losing her presence of mind in the excitement of the moment, said, "Let us alone, it is needful that we chastise these people, for they are worse than Mohammedans." Hearing this the guards became very angry and forced their way through the people by beating and kicking them until the place of burial was reached.

The Rev. Absalom preached the funeral sermon in the cemetery, in the Turkish language, so that it could be understood by the guards.

When the guards returned to their quarters, they reported the purport of the sermon to the Pasha ; and also related to him every thing concerning the disgraceful conduct of the people.

Being greatly displeased at these acts of mob violence, he sent the police to summon the Bishop into his presence. When the Bishop appeared before him, he angrily arose and pointing to his seat, thus addressed this dignitary by saying, "Come, and occupy my place, since I am supposed to me no more worthy to rule this people," thus uttering a most powerful rebuke. The Bishop fell upon his knees and in tears promised the Pasha that he would henceforth do all in his power to subdue the people from further violence and persecution. After this the Bishop at every Sunday service instructed his people to be peaceful and quiet.

In the evening of the same day upon which the funeral of Azaryan took place, Rev. Absalom preached in the house of Nergararian, taking for his text 2nd Cor. 6: 17, 18: "Wherefore come out from among them, and be ye separate, saith the Lord, and touch not the unclean *thing;* and I will receive you, And will be a father unto you, and ye shall be my sons and daughters, saith the Lord Almighty." There being a candidate for baptism, he also discoursed from Rom. 6: 4. After services several brethren remained with him during the night, for it was thought that it was not safe for him to remain alone, his nerves having been more or less effected from the trouble and excitement of the day. He remarked to Hajy Melkon that he was afraid this day would cause him his life.

Early the next morning, these brethren accompanied him to the wharf where he took a boat for Constantinople. Soon afterward he was taken very ill. From this attack he never rallied. It was thought by some* that his death was caused by the terrible experience of that day of excitement and fear, when Azaryan was buried.

Thus passed away the first native pastor of the first organized church in Turkey, from his early labors, to reap his reward in the haven of eternal rest. His loss was greatly felt by his sorrowing brethren, for he was a most earnest and successful laborer in this new open field, where he was so much needed.

*He had a like experience in Constantinople and it was thought that each of these events had something to do with his illness.

CHAPTER XI.

Previous to this time, an Armenian young man was beheaded in Constantinople by the Turkish authorities on account of changing his religion. His head was placed under him, instead of under the arm pits, according to an established custom, as an act of contempt, or as an insult to Christianity; and he was thus exposed to the public gaze for several days. The Turks treated the matter very lightly by calling him a *Giaour* (Infidel), and said, "What signifies that?" "He is nothing at all." This event very much aroused the feelings of the foreign Christian ambassadors who, through the English ambassador,* demanded of the Turkish government, that religious liberty be at once accorded to all the people, and threatened it with grave consequences should this demand not be granted.

Upon the reception of this demand, Sultan Abdoul Mejid at once issued a firman which was written in high Turkish. This language, for the most part, is made up of Arabic and Persian words and is not well understood by the common people. It was, however, interpreted to mean that his government was a temporal one; that it had no power over the souls of men; that this power belonged to God alone; and that

---

*During this period, the English ambassador, Sir Strafford Caning, was a great instrument in securing religious liberty in Turkey for native Christian subjects. With his influence he also greatly assisted the mission work.

henceforth each Christian subject of his domain should have the right to worship according to the dictates of his own conscience, and further, that no one should be permitted to call another a *Giaour*.

This firman was caused to be read in the navy yard at Nicomedia, and in every public place throughout the Sultan's dominion; namely, to Turks, Jews, Greeks, Armenians and all other nations and classes of people.

To these Protestant Christians, this was a matter for great rejoicing, and they held evening meetings for prayer and thanksgiving. In these meetings, many prayers were offered up in behalf of the Sultan and his officers.

These brethren believed that this was a direct providence of God, and that now was their opportunity to become a distinct and separate church from that of the Armenian. But having been previously advised that such an act would not be advantageous to the work, and believing that this work should also be for the good of the nation, they, after some deliberations, decided to send a petition together with their confession of faith to the Patriarch, stating that, if they could remain with them as one people without being compelled to sacrifice their belief and faith, they would rather do so, in as much as the thought of separation caused them much grief and pain.

On the 22nd of Jan., 1846, they sent to the Patriarch a letter with the above statements, together with their confession of faith which reads as follows:—

"MOST AUGUST SIR:

In these days of persecution, deprivation, slander, and injury, we are constrained to send this our petition to your Highness, for unto whom else can we go? Should we not appeal to our beloved nation, which supposes us to be its enemies, separates us from the church and your authority, and deprives us the privilege of membership, and because we are at present regarded as infidels and heretics, it is thought right and just to curse and anathematize us ? We therefore feel ourselves constrained to present this our ortho- dox confession to you for your worthy consideration.

"We confess and believe in the Holy Trinity, one Triune God, the Father, Son, and Holy Ghost; one Dominion, one Will, one Sovereign.

"We believe in Our Lord Jesus Christ as perfect God and man, and we confess Him as being the only Savior of the world, the true High Priest, mediator, intercessor, and the true Head of the church.

"We believe that He will come to judge the living and the dead, to reward them justly, giving everlasting life to the righteous, and never ending punishment to the wicked.

"We believe in the Holy Ghost, and in a perfect God, the source of truth spoken of in the law of Moses, by the pro- phets and apostles; that He is the teacher and comforter of Christian believers.

"We believe the Holy Bible, both the Old and the New Testament Scriptures, which are the canons of the church, in which is contained all doctrines and sacrament acceptable to us with all our hearts, and herein do we try to exercise our- selves to a 'conscience void of offense to God and Man." Acts 24 : 16.

"We believe that it is the duty of ourselves and of all Christians, to baptize in the name of the Holy Trinity—the Father, Son, and Holy Ghost; also that it is our duty to com- memorate the sufferings of our Lord Jesus Christ, by receiv- ing the Holy Sacrament according to the manner in which

Christ instituted it. Should you desire to further examine our faith, we confess it to be according to the Gospel which our church receives as the true word.

"We also accept the Apostolic Creed as being in harmony with the Gospel, thus declaring that our faith accords with the orthodox confession of the universal church. Therefore, we confess openly that our faith is the teaching of the Gospel as it ought to be and truly is. How then can we comply with those demands which are against the teachings of the Holy Word, and which are entirely forbidden by a curse.

"Because we would not receive those things which are not approved of in the Bible, we are regarded as being obstinate, and as apostate, and as enemies of the nation, and destroyers of the church; although we were never of this mind, but we love our nation as Paul says, 'For I could wish that myself were accursed from Christ for my brethren, my kinsmen according to the flesh.'

"To be called a Haig (Armenian), we esteem a great honor, and never assumed any other name, although we are generally called Protestants, we again confess that we are Haigs by nation, and by faith Christians, and obedient subjects to the Ottoman empire.

"Nevertheless, if we have erred in religious and civil matters—for we are not infallible—we are ready to be corrected, if you are willing to show wherein we have erred. But conviction of human nature must be done by the proof of truth, and not by force and the fear of man. We can not operate against conscience; therefore we beseech that this our declaration will be acceptable in the sight of your Majesty, and that you will have pity upon us and save us from these troubles, and we shall ever be the servants and well-wishers of your Holiness."

This confession and petition was refused by the Patriarch who said, "The cannons of the church are immutable, hence you must receive the confession of the church or we can not receive you."

Being thus cut off from the mother church, they thought with Paul, "Be ye not unequally yoked together with unbelievers." "And what agreement hath the temple of God with idols,"—"wherefore," they thought, "come out from among them and be ye separate." They now appealed to the Sultan for his royal protection over them as a distinct and separate people. The Sultan granted their petition, and issued a special firman, in which they were acknowledged as a separate church and nation, and which also granted them special privileges with other nations, and vouchsafed the protection of his dominion over them.

The following is a copy of the firman :—

PROTESTANT CHARTER OF 1847.

"*To His Excellency The Pashah Comptroller of the City Revenue :*

Whereas, The Christian subjects of the Ottoman Government professing Protestantism have experienced difficulty and embarrassments from not being hitherto under a special and separate jurisdiction and naturally the Patriarch and the Heads of the sects from which they have separated not being able to superintend their affairs ; and

Whereas, It is in contravention to the supreme will of his Imperial Majesty, our Gracious Lord and Benefactor (may God increase him in years and power), animated, as he is, with feelings of deep interest and clemency towards all classes of his subjects, that any of them should be subjected to grievance ; and

Whereas, The aforesaid Protestants, in conformity with the creed professed by them, do form a separate community :

It is his Imperial Majesty's supreme will and command, that, for the sole purpose of facilitating their affairs and of securing the welfare of said Protestants, the administration thereof should be hence-forward confided to Your Excellency, together with the allotment of the taxes to which they are subjected by law; that you do keep a separate register of their births and deaths in the bureau of your department, according to the system observed with regard to the Latin subjects; that you do issue passports and permits of marriage, and that any person of established character and good conduct chosen by them to appear as their Agent at the Porte for the transaction and settlement of their current affairs, be duly appointed for that purpose.

Such are the Imperial Commands, which you are to obey to the letter.

But although passports and the allotment of taxes are placed under special regulations which cannot be infringed upon, you will be careful that, in pursuance of his Majesty's desire, no taxes be exacted from the Protestants for permits of marriage and registration; that any necessary assistance and facility be afforded to them in their current affairs; that no interference whatever be permitted in their temporal or spiritual concerns on the part of the Patriarch, monks, or priests of other sects; but that they be enabled to exercise the profession of their creed in security, and that they be not molested one iota, either in that respect, or in any other way whatever."

Nov. 15, 1847.

The following is also a copy of the

IMPERIAL PROTESTANT CHARTER OF 1850.

"To my Vizier, Mohammed Pashah, Minister of Police at my Capital, the honorable Minister and glorious Counsellor, the Model of the World, and Regulator of the Affairs of the Community, who, directing the public interests with sublime prudence, consolidating the structure of the Empire with wisdom, and strengthening the columns of its prosperity and renown, is the recipient of every grace from the Most High· May God prolong his glory.

When this Sublime and August Mandate reaches you, let it be known that,

Whereas, Hitherto those of my Christian subjects who have embraced the Protestant faith have suffered inconvenience and difficulties, in consequence of their not being placed under a separate and special jurisdiction, and in consequence of the Patriarchs and Primates of their old creeds, which they have abandoned, naturally not being able to administer their affairs; and

Whereas, In necessary accordance with my Imperial compassion, which extends to all classes of my subjects, it is contrary to my Imperial pleasure that any one class of them should be exposed to trouble; and

Whereas, By reason of their faith, the above-mentioned already form a separate community, it is, therefore, my Royal compassionate will, that, by all means, measures be adopted for facilitating the administration of their affairs, so that they may live in peace, quiet, and security.

Let, then, a respectable and trustworthy person, acceptable to and chosen by themselves, from among their own number, be appointed, with the title of "Agent of the Protestants," who shall be attached to the department of the Minister of Police.

It shall be the duty of the Agent to have under his charge the register of the members of the community, which shall be kept at the police. The Agent shall cause to be registered therein all births and deaths in the community. All applications for passports and marriage licenses, and special transactions of the community, that are to be presented to the Sublime Porte, or to any other department, must be given under the official seal of this Agent.

For the execution of my will, this, my Royal Mandate and August Command, has been specially issued and granted from my Imperial chancery.

Hence, thou, the minister above named, in accordance with the explanations given, will execute to the letter the preceding ordinance; except that, as the collection of capitation tax, and the delivery of passports are subjected to specific regulations, you will not do anything contrary to them. You will not permit any thing to be required of them, on pretence of fees or expenses, for marriage licenses or registration.

You will see to it that, like the other communities of the Empire, in all their affairs, and in all matters appertaining to their cemeteries and places of worship, they should have every facility and needed assistance. You will not permit that any of the other communities should in any way interfere with their rites, or with their religious concerns; and, in short, in no wise with any of their affairs, secular or religious; that thus they may be enabled to exercise the usages of their faith in security.

And it is enjoined upon you not to allow them to be molested an iota in these particulars, or in any others, and that all attention and perseverance be put in requisition to maintain them in quiet and security. And in case of necessity, they are permitted to make representations regarding their affairs through their Agent to the Sublime Porte.

When this, my Imperial will, shall be brought to your knowledge and appreciation, you will have this August Edict registered in the proper department, and cause it to be perpetuated in the hands of the above-mentioned subjects, and you will see to it that its requirements be always executed in their full import.

Thus be it known to thee, and respect my sacred signet.

Written in the holy month of Moharrem, A. H. 1267 (November, 1850).

Given in the protected city of Constantinople."

CHAPTER XII.

Until now, the need of separate churches or houses of worship, schools, cemeteries, &c., had never occurred to them, much less the support of ministers, teachers, and national representatives to protect them in their rights before the Turkish government, and a station wherein these representatives should reside, together with the payment of various taxes, duties, and tribute money to the government, to say nothing about the support of their poor.

Thus placed in peculiarly trying circumstances, they were surrounded with many temptations. The religious system which was greatly cherished by them, wielded its influence against them. Even their friends and former ecclesiastics regarded them as outcasts. It is true that open persecutions had ceased since they were under the protection of the government, yet those who had hitherto been employed as mechanics, and in various other ways, were compelled to seek employment in strange cities. Many thus situated, ran well for a time, but being surrounded by a thousand worldly influences, the word of life was choked in them, and they continued no more in the narrow path. But he who was deeply interested in the truth, stood firm upon the mighty rock of salvation, through these sore troubles, and bitter hardships

59

against the numerous trials and temptations with which their paths were beset.

Under these trying circumstances, through the influence of the good Missionaries, the hand of charity was extended to them, from the Christian aid societies of America, and in this way they were enabled to build common houses of worship, which also served the purpose of schools.

Strange to say that notwithstanding many bitter persecutions, these schools found favor among the people, and many of the best Armenian families sent their children to them. This the Priests tried to oppose, but they were answered by those of their flocks who patronized those schools, that since their children had been attending them, they were not heard to blaspheme, or known to lie, and showed far greater obedience than before (what a powerful rebuke to their own system of morals!), all this showing that, although outwardly persecuted, there was a growing sentiment of respect for Protestantism.

The Bible now being made accessible to the people, began to be read, and many questions arose in their minds. These were much discussed and were often referred to the priests during their pastoral visits, but these were unable to give satisfactory answers to these questions. A lady upon a certain occasion referred a question to the priest of her parish, but he was unable to answer it. He afterwards referred to the matter in the presence of a number of other officials by whom he was at the time surrounded, and angrily asked, "Of the few who attend the Protestant chnrch, do you for a moment imagine that even all those are Protestants?" "Nay, more," was the reply, "our houses, our homes are full of them and their books."

CHAPTER XIII.

The Missionaries at this period of their work, were not only more energetic in the administration of the word of life to this new flock, but they had a special zeal to better their condition temporally. By a prudent and judicial management of their work, they demonstrated to the people that Christianity does not only make people morally better, but that it improves their temporal condition. Under their immediate instruction and care, were produced several well educated native ministers, whom they highly respected, as *earnest coworkers* in God's heritage. They also had great sympathy with their flocks, and greatly *cherished* those who were born to them in the Gospel. By the native Christians, Dr. Goodell was called their father; Dr. Hamlin, their second Illuminator. Dr. Smith was also greatly revered and loved by them.

At the time when the cholera made its appearance in Turkey, Dr. Smith, in his last visit to Nicomedia, fearing for the safety of her people, instructed the brethren in the use of the remedies and preventatives of this terrible plague. Shortly after he went to Aintap, from which place the sad news was received that he was called away from his earthly labors to his heavenly rest. It was supposed that he had fallen a victim of this dread disease. This caused much grief and sadness in the hearts of the native brethren.

CHAPTER XIV.

Directly opposite of Nicomedia, across an arm of the sea, there is a village named Bardizag, containing about 1200 Armenian families. Garabed Nergararian was several times sent by the brethren to preach to the people of this village, but they would not even permit him to enter the place, much less to preach to them. Zeparar Harutiun, the father of the writer, upon one occasion met with a certain man from that village. This man boasted to Harutiun that only city people, because of their surroundings, were liable to fall into the ways of infidelity, heresies, and false doctrines, but that the people of his village, being remote from such evil influences, remained incorruptible in the holy religion of the Church, and hence, that it was impossible for Protestantism to gain a fast hold there. Harutiun replied, "Were your people indifferent and careless as to religious matters. I should also think as you, but, for the very reason which you assign, Protestantism will be all the sooner embraced by them, and will become more powerful there than even in the cities."

Soon after this G. Nergararian, though with much difficulty, succeeded in opening a door to the work. He was followed by Megerditch, Harutiun, and several other brethren, who made it their custom to cross over to the village of Saturday evenings and hold secret meetings in the vineyard of the Suliyan Brothers. A great revival soon followed their labors. Notwithstanding the fact that G. Nergararian was frequently refused audience before, a good work was nevertheless accomplished here. The Missionaries also visited the place from time to time, and greatly aided in advancing the work. Among the many who embraced Protestantism, was a brother of Meger Oglu, the chief or principal man of the village. He was called Amuja (uncle) by the people, because he was a brother to the chief who was regarded as a father, and also because he was an aged man and greatly respected.

He at once began an earnest work amongst his people, instructing them, and selling them Bibles, religious books, and tracts which were furnished by the Missionaries. It was no unusual thing to see him upon the streets, in the public places, with his basket of books in one hand, and his open Bible in the other, crying, "The law of the Lord is perfect, converting the soul: the testimony of the Lord is sure, making wise the simple. . . . More to be desired are they than gold, yea, than much fine gold; sweeter also than honey and the honeycomb." "Boys, 'search the Scriptures, for in them ye have eternal life.'"

The street boys would often mock him crying, "Amujan hodadz khamci, gedzakghagor," (Uncle has rotten sardines for sale, uncle has rotten sardines for sale). Being deaf, he could not understand them.

A large congregation was now formed, some of the members having been formerly most strict members of the Armenian church.

The meetings were usually held in the house of one of

63

the Suliyan Brothers, but the congregation by this time became very large, and it was evident that a more commodious place of worship must be found. Rev. Dr. Hamlin and Mr. Minasyan, an Armenian gentleman who now resides in America, came to their relief and built them a church.

In this connection it will not be out of place to state that these noble hearted men also spent a large sum of money in establishing and erecting a church at Broosa.

CHAPTER XV.

Once two students were sent from the Babak seminary to a village of about 400 Armenian families, for the purpose of preaching to the people and selling and distributing to them religious books and tracts. The name of this village is Ovajuk and is near to Bardizag. After being there a short time, they took a stroll to the top of a beautiful hill near by the village. Upon this hill was built a little chapel devoted to the Prophet Elijah, in which was placed a picture of the Prophet. Soon after they had returned from the chapel, two women reported in the village that these two Protestants had defaced and desecrated Elijah's image. This story was very soon circulated through the entire village, and the women becoming greatly excited, rushed upon them and beat them with clubs, hoe-handles and whatever else they could lay hold of, nearly tearing their clothes to pieces. Their books and tracts they tore up into fragments and scattered them upon the streets. The two men barely escaped with their lives, and concealed themselves in a ditch under some bushes, in a field not far from the village, where they remained until they found an opportunity to make their way back to Nicomedia.

65

After the excitement of the villagers had been somewhat allayed, they began to see the folly of their course, and fearing that it might cause them much trouble, they laid the mater before their Bishop and appealed to him to help them out of the difficulty into which their rashness had led them. He therefore went to the Pasha and bribed him to quash the case, should it be brought before the court.

The Protestant representative of Nicomedia presented the matter for trial, but the Pasha delayed it from time to time, and finally treated it with indifference. Seeing that it was impossible to obtain justice in the case, the Missionary of Nicomedia referred it to the English Ambassador at Constantinople. Through his influence at the Sublime Porte at Constantinople, his interpreter, Mr. Brown, an English gentleman, a very brave and noble looking man, together with the Kavass (Pasha's guard), was sent by a special steamer to Nicomedia to make an investigation of it.

When Mr. Brown stated the object of his visit, to the Pasha, who seeing that it was likely to assume a serious aspect before the government and involve him in great difficulty, most willingly agreed to an investigation, and at once summoned the national representative from that village. The result was that a number of the parties who were implicated in the affair, were imprisoned for a short time, and the villagers were compelled to pay damages covering the loss of books, tracts, etc.

From this time on, the severe persecutions and the great obstacles which heretofore had so much prevented the spreading of God's holy kingdom, began to disappear, and the life giving principles of Christianity everywhere showed signs of spreading all over the country.

66

In ten years not only at Nicomedia and surrounding country had a glorious work been accomplished, but all over the country had the blessed seeds of the Gospel been scattered. In many native homes the Bible was found translated in their own mother tongue. Many churches had been established in succession throughout all Asia Minor.

CHAPTER XVI.

Once the Rev. Dr. Dwight went into a certain town in Armenia to preach to the people and distribute books amongst them. This was soon reported to the Vicar Bishop named Bedros, who strictly commanded his people to have no communication with him whatever. He also instituted a bitter persecution against Dr. Dwight, so that he could obtain neither food, lodging, nor even food for his horse. This Vartabed,* or Bishop, demanded of his people that they gather up all the books and tracts which had been distributed amongst them. When these were collected and brought to him, he burnt them in the church yard, in the presence of the people, but being prompted out of mere curiosity to know what they contained, he secretly retained one of each kind to read. After perusing them carefully, he was finally convinced of the doctrines and truths which they taught, and at once ceased to persecute the Protestants. He also began to exhibit signs of friendship towards them and would sometimes secretly invite them into his own private room. This soon became known to his parishioners who began to chide him for his acts of kindness and leniency toward Protestants, and finally waged a fierce persecution against him, so that at last he was obliged to flee to

---

*A vartabed is a collegeman whose business is to preach and to teach the people.

68

Constantinople where he threw dimself under the protection of Stephen Effendi, the Protestant representative before the Turkish Sublime Porte. Having in the meantime become a truly converted man, he was sent to the brethren at Nicomedia, where he might be safe from danger or harm.

Here he married a widow lady, and in time they were blessed with a little boy. It was Dr. Dwight's happy privilege to baptize this little child. The writer well remembers the impressive words uttered upon that occasion. Standing in the altar he spoke as follows :

"God's providence is wonderful! His word is sharper than a two edged sword, penetrating the most obdurate heart. How wonderful are his ways! This Vartabed (pointing to the man) was once my greatest persecutor, not even permitting his people to give me provender for my horse. But now, how changed! What a blessed work have the truths of the Gospel wrought upon his heart! To-day he brings his child to me for Christian baptism. If we but live faithful to our calling and obey God's holy law, we shall yet see greater wonders than these." etc.

This man was *very rich* while filling his official station in the Church as a Vartabed ; but in accepting the true doctrines of Christianity, he was compelled to leave it all, and hence for the sake of Christ's holy religion, he became very poor, so that he was necessitated to sell vegetables upon the street corners in order that he and his family might live.

One day, an Armenian gentleman, who knew how this Vartabed had formerly been honored in the Church, accidentally recognized him as he was engaged in his usual occupation. This man having great sympathy for him, went to him, and said, "I am greatly surprised to see you in this condition, and am grieved at the thought of it. Once you were highly honored by the Church as a beloved Vartabed, wearing upon you the Sacerdotal robes, the insignia of your sacred office. Acolytes and Priests served you. Your hands were kissed by your loving parishioners, and into them money, without stint, was permitted to fall. But now how different, how degraded! Why such a condition of things? I pity you, I pity your wit."

He meekly answered, "For the sake of the Gospel truth, for the sake of my immortal soul, and for the *reformation* of my people, I will do even worse things, if such be required of me." What a noble self-sacrificing spirit!

His little child who was baptized by Dr. Dwight, is now a man in the prime of life, and to-day he is an honored citizen of the United States of America.

CHAPTER XVII.

From what has been said concerning the persecutions of the Protestant Christians in this brief history, it must not be understood that the Armenians are a hostile and unkind people, imperceptible to the truth, and enemies to the Christian religion. But as we have many times learned of the early Christians, how they were persecuted from a blind zeal and ignorance on the part of their persecutors, as even in the case of St. Paul before his miraculous conversion, so these brethren were persecuted by their own people—oftentimes by their own kindred—who thought they were doing the *will* of God. When the Missionaries came to Turkey, they were kindly received by the Patriarch and clergymen who showed great hospitality and favor to them, and encouraged them to build up schools which they promised to support, by sending to these their young men and priests to be educated. But afterwards the Jesuits, who are ever the uncompromising enemies of Protestantism, secretly stirred up the Armenian and Greek leaders against the Missionaries and their work, whom they now began to regard with suspicion and envy. Even among the Armenian Priests and collegemen were those who, though they at first persecuted the Protestants, became not only their staunchest friends, but also earnest workers for the cause of Christ.

71

The Armenians are a most kind and hospitable people, and for this very reason the Missionaries have labored among them with far greater success than in any other nation in Turkey. To them the name of Christ was not new. The seeds of Christianity were, in the beginning, sowed in Armenia. Indeed, the Armenian Church lays claim to Apostolic origin, hence they were the first to embrace Christianity as a nation in the third century. About the year 410, the Bible was translated into the Armenian language.

At a very early age the Armenian nation was inclined to civilization more than any other nation in the East. The archives of Nineveh are said to have yielded some of its rich treasures to the nation, in the time of the Parthian, Vagharshaeges, about a century and a half before Christ. They are an interesting people and have a literature peculiarly their own, which is noted for its deep thought and classical refinement. Many ancient works, mostly manuscripts, have, at different times, been brought to light, and are said to be very valuable. One of England's great poets makes mention of several very learned works, of which he speaks very highly. Some of these have since been translated into French, and are greatly admired by the learned. He also alludes to several other interesting books. Many valuable manuscripts yet remain locked up in the Monasteries in that country, which, if brought to light, would, no doubt, contribute much to ancient or Biblical history. Their ancient theological writings are especially fine and are behind that of no other nation in point of deep learning and sound Christian doctrine.

Their religious literature is pervaded by a deep Christian sentiment, a pious spirit, and a Christian zeal worthy of imitation. They were also characterized for their missionary

72

spirit; for we learn from their writings that they had taught the doctrines of Christianity as far as Hindostan. For these principles they were frequently persecuted, many of them being compelled to suffer martyrdom; they were frequently led into war with the Persians and others on account of these things. The doubly barbarous Persians, their most bloodthirsty enemies, were particularly troublesome neighbors to them, since they wished to force them to deny Christianity and accept the teachings of Zoroaster, or *Fire Worship*. Persecuted at first by the Persians and others on the one hand, and afterwards by the Turks on the other, they were constrained to forego their civil power rather than that they should lose the Christian religion. It is, indeed, a miracle that they, to-day, bear a Christian name at all. Is it not rather a wonder that their history was not buried in oblivion and long ago forgotten? Their oppressors were cruel and barbarous, especially the Persians and Turks who knew no brounds to their cruelty, often tying the aged in pairs and then splitting them in halves. Infants were snatched from their mothers' breasts and massacred in the presence of these terror stricken mothers. Nay more, the bowels of the pregnant were even ripped open and their unborn babes destroyed before their expiring eyes. Thus the land of their nativity was consecrated with their life blood. And all this they suffered for the sake of the Christian religion. For this cause they were forced to part with their beautiful daughters who were brutally treated and desecrated by their oppressors.

It is true that they, as a church, have since become corrupted, but this gradually came from their associations with the Greeks and Romans, whose superstitions crept into the Church during their terrible struggles in those dark ages.

Although the Armenian nation in part to-day is held in subjugation by the authority of a miserable government, it is the life of Turkey. Were it not for this circumstance, they would compare favorably with other enlightened nations of the civilized world. As it is, they are entirely cut off and separated from all other enlightened peoples. They have great capacity for improvement and only lack the opportunity. Among them is a great desire for improvement, and many of their young men are going abroad to seek after the knowledge which they so much wish. Not a few of them have been lead to seek this improvement in America, since the United States offers such great opportunities to those who thirst after wisdom.

If the Missionaries ever become successful in the evangelization of Turkey, they can only accomplish this through the Armenian nation, since the Mohammedans are unapproachable, while the Greeks, like many, who in the time of Christ boasted themselves to be the children of Abraham, claim to have taught to the world philosophy, science, and refinement, through Aristotle, Socrates, Plato, and Homer; nay more, they boast that their nation gave birth to the early Church Fathers, who spread Christianity abroad through the Earth.

Once a Greek proudly boasted to the writer, saying, "We have given you Philosophy and the Fathers of the Church, and have taught Christianity to the world, now do you Protestants presume to teach us?" He replied, "It is true you have given to the world philosophers and the early Church Fathers and taught it Christianity, but the Europeans and Americans have robbed you of your learning and piety, and left you nothing but your pride and vanity. What is the profit to you, if your great great grandfather was rich and left

74

you poverty stricken? Your church has long since lost its spiritual life and is now sunken into superstition."

The Greeks do not recognize any rites or doctrines except their own as canonical, and they never received any one from another church without baptizing him.

We are, however, glad to say that there are, at present, quite a number of young men from the Greek nation, who are attending some of the Missionary seminaries, and who give promise of much good for the future. Upon these rests the hope of success in converting the Greeks to Protestantism, for though they be proud and haughty, they will receive the Gospel when it is brought to them by those of their own nation.

CHAPTER XVIII.

From the Babak Seminary, through the direct influence and care of Dr. Hamlin, had gone forth many highly educated and earnest native ministers who accomplished a good work among their people to the glory and honor of God.

Through the Female Boarding School established by the Missionaries at Constantinople under the care of Dr. Goodell, much good was also done. The native ladies who graduated here, rendered much efficient aid, and have been great instruments in the hands of the Missionaries in advancing the work of saving souls.

At this time the Armenian Patriarch occupied a seat in the Sublime Porte at Constantinople, as the nation's representative before the Turkish government; his brother, Stephen Effendi, held a like position as the Protestant representative.

In the Armenian nation, a great thirst for knowledge was awakened, and there was a glorious expectation for the future, both on the part of the Missionaries and the native Christians as may be shown from the following taken from "Forty Years in the Turkish Empire," pages 299 and 382 which says, "If this work of God goes forward in the same proportion for ten years to come, as it has gone for ten years past, there will be no further occasion for any of us to remain here, unless it be to assist you in bringing to a knowledge of these same precious saving doctrines of the Gospel, the Greeks and Jews and others around you. . . . .

"We have been spared to see great and wonderful changes, since Mrs. Goodell and myself came to this Eastern world, a third of a century ago. But those who come after us will see still greater; and herein do we rejoice; yea, and we hope, by the mercy of our Lord Jesus Christ to rejoice for being sinners saved by grace alone."

These things not only gave them great hope and joy, and encouraged them in their labors, but these were glorious tidings to the American Christians, and the American Board soon became a mighty society which shed a wonderful influence abroad among other Christian denominations so that they, too, began to imbibe a Missionary spirit.

But more than a half century has passed since the Missionaries commenced their work in Turkey; have their hopes and great expectations been fully realized? And have the native brethren enjoyed the fruits of their bitter trials and persecutions, for themselves and their offspring? We are obliged to answer sadly, NO.

In this brief history, it is not the purpose of the writer to explain the many causes which have retarded the realization of these high expectations, suffice it to say that what *those* good Missionaries sowed, they reaped.

We read in the Revelations that to St. John was given a little book, which in his mouth was sweet as honey, but which, when he had swallowed it, became *bitter*. It is indeed true that when the word of God is received in the heart, it causes His people many severe trials within, and not unfrequently bitter persecutions without; but again it is also true that in the mouth it is *sweet*, enlightening the understanding and purifying the heart, reforming individual families and nations, helping them to raise above sin and degredation, causing nations to enjoy the highest civilization, and above all, giving them the hope of Glory in which they can trust in life and in death, and causing this hope to be their great support in the day of adversity, yea, that blessed hope which awaits the glorious appearing of our Lord and Savior Jesus Christ with all His holy saints.

Thank God that he has a chosen people who, bringing forth fruits of His glorious righteousness, shine as lights into the ends of the dark corners of the earth, imparting to them the light and life which they have received from their Heavenly Master.

For those who have already labored faithfully and successfully, but who have since gone to their rest, what an unspeakable joy do they now share together with many of those for whom they so earnestly labored, in our Father's house above ! Once they sowed in tears, now they are reaping with rejoicing. They are numbered with those "which came out of great tribulation, and have washed their robes, and made them white in the blood of the Lamb."

When we cast our pennies into the mission treasury or tract society, we may not always see the blessed results from our labors of love, but after a short time, when our work is done, and we enter our eternal home, the Heavenly Kingdom, *there* we shall see great multitudes from all nations, "from the east and from the west, and from the north, and from the south," with Abraham, Isaac and Jacob, singing hallelujahs of salvation, who have been saved by these humble means.

What a pleasant thought for the contemplation of a Christian to know that not only he himself will be happily saved in that beautiful world, but that he has also, by his labors, been the means of turning many souls to righteousness whereby they too may have eternal life. In *this* way only will they have secured the great object of their being, and then will they not have lived in vain. Then will be enjoyed the glorious promises of our dear Savior through all eternity. If even the giving of a cup of cold water shall not be without its reward, then how much *more blessed* will be reward of those who have been the humble means of saving souls for whom Christ has died.

"And they that be wise, shall shine as the brightness of the firmament : and they that turn many to righteousness, as the stars for ever and ever." "Yea, saith the spirit, that they may rest from their labors; and their works do follow them." "Well done thou good and faithful servant, enter thou into the joys of the Lord."

"Therefore, my beloved brethren, be ye steadfast, unmovable, always abounding in the work of the Lord, forasmuch as ye know that your labor is not in vain in the Lord." 1 Cor. 15 : 58.

> "How happy are the Saints above,
> Who once went sorrowing here;
> But now they taste unmingled love,
> And joy without a tear."

www.ingramcontent.com/pod-product-compliance
Lightning Source LLC
Chambersburg PA
CBHW022142090426
42742CB00010B/1351